PERU

Anna Cavallo

Lerner Publications Company • Minneapolis

Lerner Publications Company
A division of Lerner Publishing Group, Inc.
241 First Avenue North
Minneapolis, MN 55401 U.S.A.

Website address: www.lernerbooks.com

Library of Congress Cataloging-in-Publication Data

Cavallo, Anna.
　　Peru / by Anna Cavallo.
　　　　p.　cm. — (Country explorers)
　　Includes index.
　　ISBN 978–0–7613–6416–0 (lib. bdg. : alk. paper)
　　　　1. Peru—Juvenile literature. I. Title.
　　F3408.5.C375　2012
　　985—dc22　　　　　　　　　　　2011000984

Manufactured in the United States of America
1 – MG – 7/15/11

Table of Contents

Welcome!

Let's explore Peru! This country sits on the west coast of the South American continent. Ecuador and Colombia are to the north of Peru. Brazil and Bolivia lie to the east of Peru. Chile sits to the south. The Pacific Ocean washes Peru's western shores.

equator

Peru

The beautiful blue waters of the Pacific Ocean lap against Peru's coastline.

N

ECUADOR

COLOMBIA

BRAZIL

LOW SELVA

AMAZON
RIVER

Iquitos

MARANON
RIVER

HUALLAGA
RIVER

HIGH SELVA

PERU

ANDES MOUNTAINS

UCAYALI
RIVER

Lima ★

PACIFIC
OCEAN

Ollantaytambo

Machu
Picchu ⁂

MADRE DE DIOS
RIVER

• Cuzco

BOLIVIA

Lake
Titicaca

Puno •

MOUNT
AMPATO

Arequipa •

MILES
0   100   200   300

0   100   200   300   400
KILOMETERS

CHILE

	mountains
	high selva
	low selva (rain forest)
	volcano
⁂	ancient ruins
★	country's capital
•	city

5

The Coast

The land along Peru's western edge is mainly flat. Some of Peru's biggest cities sit near the coast.

Lima, Peru's capital city, sits at the top of a cliff overlooking the Pacific. East of Lima is a stretch of flat land.

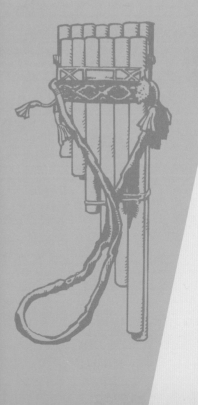

Farmworkers harvest rice in northwestern Peru. Rice grows well on the flat land near the coast.

People living here enjoy mild weather. Temperatures range from about 60° to 80°F (16° to 26°C). The coast gets very little rain. Still, much of Peru's farming is done here. Fishing is also big business along the coast.

Magnificent Mountains

The jagged peaks and high plains (flat lands) of the Andes Mountains cover about one-third of Peru. This area is also known as the highlands. The weather in the highlands is cooler. Winter often brings freezing temperatures. Rain falls during the warmer months, from November to April.

The highest peaks of the Andes are snow covered year-round.

Lake Titicaca sits on Peru's southern border with Bolivia. This lake is the largest in Peru. It is also one of the highest lakes in the world.

The Selva

The *selva* covers more than half of Peru. This is an area of rain forest. The selva is home to jaguars, monkeys, frogs, and parrots. Snakes, turtles, and many fish and birds live here too. Plants thrive in the jungle's warm, wet weather.

Bright, colorful flowers stand out against the dense green background of the rain forest.

A blue and yellow macaw makes its home in Peru's rain forest.

Not many people live in this area. Few roads wind through the thick jungle. People must travel by airplane or boat.

Map Whiz Quiz

Look at the map on page 5. Trace the outline of Peru onto a thin sheet of paper. Do you see Brazil? Mark it with an *E* for east. Find the Pacific Ocean. Label it with a *W* for west. Look for Ecuador. Mark it with an *N* for north. Next, find the country of Chile. Give it an *S* for south. Color Peru yellow. Then color the Pacific Ocean blue.

Early Peruvians

People in Peru began forming villages more than four thousand years ago. The Chavin lived in the central highlands around 800 B.C. They built temples with huge stone blocks. Later, the Paracas settled along the coast. They invented fine weaving methods.

A weaver from the Paracas culture wove this poncho with wool that had been dyed different colors.

The Nazca people lived south of Lima starting about two thousand years ago. They built an underground system to carry water to their crops. The Wari people were the first to take over other groups. Their lands covered most of modern Peru. The Wari thrived until about one thousand years ago.

The Nazca Lines

The Nazca made huge designs in the ground. The Nazca Lines form animal shapes, spirals, and other patterns. Their shapes can be seen only from an airplane. Experts still don't understand how or why the Nazca made these lines.

The Nazca created this design of a hummingbird. It is 305 feet (93 meters) from tip to tail.

The Incas

The Incas lived in the Andes Mountains about five hundred years ago. Their huge kingdom spread from Colombia to Chile. Incan workers built stone roads, bridges, temples, and homes. Farmers cut terraces (flat, narrow fields) into mountainsides. The farmers grew crops on the terraces. Workers mined gold to make jewelry. The Incas also decorated important buildings with gold.

The Incas built this structure on the side of a steep mountain in Ollantaytambo, Peru. They stored food here.

High in the mountains near Cuzco is Machu Picchu. This ancient site may have been a vacation spot for the Incan leader.

Juanita the Ice Maiden

In 1995, a scientist hiking on Mount Ampato found the frozen body of an Incan girl. She had died about five hundred years ago. Ice had kept her body and her clothes exactly the same as they were then. Scientists learned more about Incan life by studying her body. They called her Juanita the Ice Maiden.

The ruins of Machu Picchu sit high up in the Andes. Visitors can still see its terraced farm.

Modern Peru

Explorers from Spain reached Peru in 1532. They wanted the Incas' gold and land. The explorers fought the Incas. The explorers won the battle and gained control of the Incan Empire. Peru didn't declare independence from Spain until 1821.

This illustration shows the Incan leader Atahualpa kneeling before Spanish explorers in 1532.

Almost half the people in modern Peru belong to native groups. About one in three people has both Spanish and native ancestors. White people have Spanish or other European ancestors. Small numbers of people with African, Chinese, and Japanese backgrounds also live in Peru.

These girls live in Lima. Many modern Peruvians have a mix of native and European ancestors.

17

The Coast and the Highlands

Lifestyles near the coast are very different from those in the highlands. Along the coast, many people make enough money to live comfortably. Businesses, factories, and restaurants provide jobs. Most white people live near the coast.

Businesspeople take a midday break in downtown Lima.

18

Most people in the highlands belong to native groups. They grow crops and raise animals. Highland people grow enough food to feed their families. But they have little money to buy anything else. Many highlanders have moved to cities in recent years. They hope to find better jobs or to go to school.

This Quechua girl helps her family raise sheep in the highlands of southern Peru.

Farming

Sugarcane, potatoes, rice, and corn are important crops in Peru. Coffee is too. Farmers also grow cacao beans, cotton, and many fruits and vegetables. And some farmers raise llamas and alpacas for meat and wool. But only a small part of the land is fit for farming.

Peruvian farmers harvest coffee beans in southeastern Peru.

Some farmers still rely on ancient methods. For example, grains and fruit trees still grow on hillside terraces. Near Lake Titicaca, water flows in ditches between rows of raised land. Farmers used raised fields like these hundreds of years ago.

Using ancient methods, farmers plant crops on rows of raised earth. Valleys between the rows bring water to growing plants.

Capital Cities

Lima is Peru's capital city. Lima is also the largest city in Peru. The Spanish called Lima the City of Kings. About eight million people live in Lima. The city is a modern center of business and trade. But beautiful Spanish buildings from the 1600s still line some streets. Lima's museums hold many ancient treasures.

High-rise apartments and office buildings line the Pacific Ocean's shores in Lima.

Cuzco was the capital of the Incan Empire. Historic Spanish buildings and ancient Incan buildings still stand there side by side.

Hola Sarah,

Today we are visiting Arequipa. It's called the White City because lots of buildings are made from white rock. I saw Juanita the Ice Maiden in a museum here. She is frozen in a glass case. How cool!
See you soon!

Katie

Y
Y
An

Ice Maiden

Getting Around

Traveling in Peru can be hard. Steep, winding roads cut through the mountains. Small buses, called micros, run between cities. Some paths are too narrow for cars. Donkeys and llamas help people carry supplies in the highlands.

A Peruvian girl leads a pack horse along a trail in the Andes. Horses, llamas, and donkeys help carry heavy loads in the mountains.

24

Highways connect cities along the coast. These roads also run to major highland cities such as Cuzco and Arequipa. In cities, people hop into a crowded *combi* or *colectivo*. These vans travel routes as buses do. In the Amazon city of Iquitos, open-air taxis fill the streets.

Open-air taxis take passengers for rides in Iquitos.

Languages

Most people in Peru speak Spanish. But groups in the Andes still speak native languages. The most common is Quechua. This was the language of the Incas. Many Aymara people live in the south. They speak the Aymara language.

Spanish-language newspapers are for sale at this newspaper stand.

These schoolchildren in the Andes learn the Quechua language.

Saying Hello

Learn how to say some helpful phrases in Spanish and Quechua!

English	Spanish	Quechua
hello	hola	napaykullayki (NAH-pie-koo-YAH-ee-kee)
good-bye	adios	ratu kama (rah-too KAH-mah)
yes	sí	arí (ah-REE)
no	no	mana (MAH-NAH)
please	por favor	allichu (ah-YEE-choo)
thank you	gracias	yusulipayki (you-soo-lee-PIE-kee)

At Home

Many families in rural areas live in small homes. People make the homes from mud bricks. These houses may have dirt floors and tile or straw roofs. They usually don't have electricity or running water.

This house is made of dried mud bricks. A roof made of thick layers of grass keeps out the rain.

Homes on Stilts

The city of Iquitos sits on the Amazon River. Some people build homes on rafts or on stilts! That's because the river floods during the wettest months each year. The stilts and rafts keep the homes from flooding.

In cities, most people live in modern apartment buildings or houses. The poorest people live in small shacks. Families in Peru often live close together. And homes can be crowded. Adults and kids often share a bedroom.

The houses in Iquitos are made on rafts or stilts so they will stay safe when the Amazon River rises.

Food

Most Peruvian food is spicy. On the coast, people love ceviche. Cooks make this dish with raw seafood soaked in lemon or lime juice and peppers. Meat, potatoes, and quinoa seeds are common foods in the mountains. So are soups and stews.

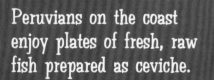

Peruvians on the coast enjoy plates of fresh, raw fish prepared as ceviche.

Cooks prepare a pachamanca. Meat and vegetables are placed on top of hot stones to cook. A pit of bricks surrounds the food. The pit will be covered with heavy, dampened cloths.

For the large midday meal, a cook might make a pachamanca. This traditional meal cooks in the ground! Meat and vegetables roast between hot stones in a pit. Cooks also serve *cuy*, or roasted guinea pig, for special meals.

Faith and Festivals

About four out of five people in Peru are Roman Catholic. The Spaniards brought this religion to Peru. But most people also worship gods from Peru's ancient cultures.

Peruvian women dance during an Easter parade.

32

The Festival of the Sun celebrates the Inca New Year. It lasts for a whole week. Many visitors travel to Cuzco in June for this colorful celebration. Peruvians honor the sun. They celebrate the days getting longer. Some people wear Incan costumes and perform special dances.

Peruvians parade through the streets of Cuzco to celebrate Inti Raymi, or the Festival of the Sun.

Time for School

Kids get up early for school. In the Andes, some students travel a long distance. They may leave home at six o'clock in the morning!

These students in the Andes wear colorful traditional clothing to school.

Children go to elementary school for six years. Then they have five years of secondary school. But poor families often need their children to work and earn money. Only about one-half of all children finish secondary school. Of those, about one in three goes to college.

These students in Lima pose for a picture in their school uniforms.

The Sounds of Peru

Huayno folk music is the traditional sound of Peru. Players use panpipes and guitarlike string instruments. *Cumbia* music blends traditional music with rock. Near Lima, black Peruvians mix Spanish music with African drum beats and native musical instruments. This music, called criollo, became popular in the 1990s.

Peruvian musicians play traditional instruments during a festival in Puno.

Let's Dance!

Dance is an important part of Peru's culture. Couples in the Andes turn, hop, and tap their feet in huayno dances. Near the coast, dancers perform the *marinera* to criollo music. They keep time by waving handkerchiefs. In the south, dancers cut the air with their arms in the "dance of the scissors." This dance includes jumps and fancy steps.

These performers dance the marinera.

A Colorful Craft

People in Peru spin wool from llamas and alpacas into thread for weaving. This thread makes very warm hats, blankets, sweaters, ponchos, and scarves.

A Peruvian woman weaves together colorful woolen threads by hand.

This family from Cuzco wears traditional, handmade clothing.

Peruvians have woven colorful cloth for thousands of years. In some places, weavers still use old-fashioned weaving methods. The patterns in the cloth may show the sun or other signs of nature.

What to Wear?

People in the Andes dress in traditional clothing. Girls wear colorful wool sweaters and layered skirts. Boys wear ponchos with patterns or designs. Most people in cities dress in modern business and casual clothes.

39

Business

Mining is an important business in Peru. The country produces much of the world's copper, silver, lead, and zinc. Farming and fishing are also big businesses. More people work in farming than in any other job. Peruvians sell coffee and other crops to many countries. Factories process food or make plastics or cloth. Near tourist areas, many people find work in restaurants or as tour guides.

Huge dump trucks move heavy loads of rock dug from this gold mine in northern Peru.

Tourism

Peru has attracted more visitors in recent years. Machu Picchu is the most popular tourist site. Peru's many national parks and reserves also draw visitors. The parks protect the land and wildlife. Tourists can explore the land in ways that don't harm the rain forest or ancient sites.

41

Sports

Soccer is popular everywhere in Peru. Fans love to play the game and to watch it on TV. Peru's national team hopes to make it to the World Cup soon.

Residents of Lima play a game of soccer.

Surfing is also popular along the Pacific coast. The national surfing contest features the country's best talent each year. Bullfighting, a Spanish tradition, still has some fans in Peru too.

A matador waves his red cape during a bullfight at a festival in southern Peru.

THE FLAG OF PERU

Peru's flag has three bands of color. The bands on the left and right sides are red. The color stands for the blood of people who died fighting for independence from Spain. The white band in the center stands for peace. The flag that the government flies includes a coat of arms, or sign of the nation. A wreath surrounds a shield. The shield is decorated with symbols of Peru's animals, plants, and minerals. Peru adopted this flag in 1825 after it gained independence from Spain.

FAST FACTS

FULL COUNTRY NAME: Republic of Peru

AREA: 496,225 square miles (1,285,217 square kilometers). That is a little smaller than the state of Alaska.

MAIN LANDFORMS: the Andes mountain range and highlands; dry coastal plains; the selva

MAJOR RIVERS: Amazon, Huallaga, Madre de Dios, Maranon, Ucayali

ANIMALS AND THEIR HABITATS: seabirds, sea lions, (Pacific coast); deer, giant turtles, iguanas (dry coastal plain); alpacas, llamas, vicunas (mountains); spectacled bear (eastern edge of Andes); crocodiles, jaguars, macaws, monkeys, river dolphins, snakes, wild boars (selva and Amazon River)

CAPITAL CITY: Lima

OFFICIAL LANGUAGES: Spanish and Quechua

POPULATION: about 29,547,000

GLOSSARY

ancestors: relatives who lived long ago

ancient: having been around for a long time; very old

capital: a city where the government is located

continent: any one of seven large areas of land. The continents are Africa, Antarctica, Asia, Australia, Europe, North America, and South America.

culture: the way of life, ideas, and customs of a particular group of people

expert: someone who knows a lot about a certain subject

highland: a high but flat area among mountains

plains: large areas of flat land

rain forest: a warm, woodland area where lots of rain falls each year and crowded treetops shade the ground

reserve: an area of land set aside to protect the plants and animals there from harm

tradition: a custom, belief, or practice that people in a particular culture pass on to one another

TO LEARN MORE

BOOKS

Hynson, Colin. *You Wouldn't Want to Be an Inca Mummy!: A One-Way Journey You'd Rather Not Make.* New York: Franklin Watts, 2008. Learn more about life in the ancient Inca Empire through this book's funny illustrations and text.

Knutson, Barbara. *Love and Roast Chicken.* Minneapolis: Carolrhoda Books, 2004. With striking art, this story tells how an Andean guinea pig outwits a fox to avoid becoming dinner.

Patent, Dorothy Hinshaw. *Llamas.* Minneapolis: Lerner Publications Company, 2002. Find out more about these gentle, woolly animals.

Wojahn, Rebecca Hogue, and Donald Wojahn. *A Rain Forest Food Chain: A Who-Eats-What Adventure in South America.* Minneapolis: Lerner Publications Company, 2009. Explore the Amazon rain forest by following three different paths in the food chain.

WEBSITES

Peru: Country Facts, Information, Photos, Videos—National Geographic Kids
http://kids.nationalgeographic.com/kids/places/find/peru/
Visit this website for photos from Peru's highlands and send an e-card.

Time for Kids around the World—Peru
http://www.timeforkids.com/TFK/kids/hh/goplaces/main/0,28375,602932,00.html
This site is packed with information. Check out a day in the life of an eleven-year-old girl in Lima, or go sightseeing around the country!

INDEX